AF489263

To all of our little tacos, we love you
with all of our hearts.
May you always remain full.

Taco woke up and looked around, he should be happy that today is his birthday but he feels so empty inside.

Taco begins getting ready for his birthday party. He puts up all the decorations.

He makes sure the cake is ready.

He blows up the balloons.

He goes over the guestlist to make sure everyone he invited is coming. Meat, Lettuce, Tomato, Guacamole, Cheese and Sour Cream have all said yes to coming.

HAPPY BIRTHDAY

All of Taco's friends are excited to go to the party, but they don't know what to get Taco for his birthday.

All the guests have arrived! The decorations are taco-mazing! There is a colorful banner, mini tacos everywhere and a cake with sprinkles!

HAPPY BIRTHDAY

Taco greets his friends with the best smile
that he can manage, but all of his friends can tell that
something is wrong.

I'm so happy that you guys came to see me.
I'm very happy to celebrate my birthday
but i feel so empty inside.
I feel like my shell is empty and I don't know how to fill it.

Taco's friends knew right then what they should get Taco for his birthday.

Please take some meat- ingful filling.

How do you feel now Taco?
A little better. Thank you!

Take one of my leaves.

Thank you! I feel a little bit better.

You're welcome!

How about a slice of Mato?
If you think It'll help.

So....?
I feel a lot better, Thank You!

A little bit of
Guac always
makes me feel
better

Thank You! You're right, a little bit of guac made me feel better.

Still feeling a little empty, maybe cheese can help?

No one can resist a
little cheese!
Take some please.

How do you feel now?
I'm feeling more like a taco now!

There's nothing sour about sharing my friendship with you.

Thank you so much!
I feel so much
better!

You're welcome!
I'm so happy we could
help you fill your shell.

They all decided that they would each give Taco
a piece of themselves to help him feel full inside.

Taco had his fillings! He was full again.
His friends gave him the best gift he could ever ask for.
He decided that this was the best birthday ever,
all because he had the best friends in the entire world.

The End

Stay tuned!

More Taco-Ventures to come!

9 798869 279613